Let's Dance!

George Ancona

HAMPTON-BROWN

Actions

kick high

turn around

reach up

dance gracefully

spin quickly

step forward

dance together

kick back

step across

Let's Dance!

If you can speak, you can sing.
If you can walk, you can dance.
All you have to do is

kick,

step,

turn,

hop,

jump,

reach,

leap,

and wiggle.

5

Fast or slow?
Listen to the music.

SAXOPHONE

TIBETAN FIDDLE

SCOTTISH BAGPIPES

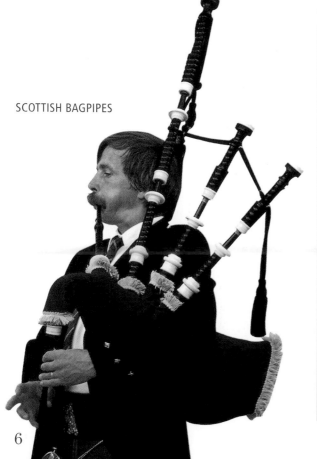

The rhythm will
tell you how to move.

CONGOLESE DRUM

BACONGO is the national dance of the Congo in Africa. It is also performed at funerals. Individual dancers step into a circle of friends and dance to the spirit of the dead.

You can
dance alone,

8

SCOTTISH COUNTRY DANCERS. This dance developed in the Lowlands of Scotland and was influenced by early French, Italian, and English dancing. The footwork is complicated and lively.

with a friend,

or with a whole bunch of people.

CIRCLE FOLK DANCE.
Young people at a summer camp join hands in a joyful unrehearsed dance.

Dancing is a way of celebrating.

CHINESE LION DANCE. This dance is performed to celebrate the New Year to the accompaniment of crashing cymbals and bursting firecrackers.

ENGLISH MORRIS DANCERS perform during a springtime ceremony. The bells on their legs are to wake up the earth so it will receive the seeds in the spring planting.

There are dances that celebrate the seasons.

PUEBLO HARVEST DANCE. In the fall, Native Americans of the Southwest pueblos celebrate the season with a dance that gives thanks for a good harvest.

SEVILLANAS.
A flamenco dance from Spain has Gypsy and Moorish origins. The guitarists are accompanied by singers who also clap to accentuate the rhythm of the music.

Dances from the old countries

THE JARANA is a dance from the Yucatan peninsula of Mexico. It is a blend of Spanish and native Mayan rhythms. The women wear white *huipiles* with colorful embroidery. The men dress all in white.

were brought to the New World.

People dress up
to dance in their
traditional clothes.

GREEK FOLK DANCERS

POWWOW FANCY DANCER

POLYNESIAN DANCER

MATACHINE DANCER

MEXICAN HAT DANCERS

KOREAN FAN DANCER

19

Children dance in their parents' footsteps.

PUEBLO HARVEST DANCE

CONTRA DANCE

Over time, dances change.

CLOG DANCING originated in northern England, where miners would dance with their wooden shoes. Their descendants who settled in the Appalachian mountains continued the tradition.

TAP DANCING developed from clog dancing. It mixes Irish, English, African, and Native American styles together. Instead of clogs, tap dancers wear shoes with metal taps on the heels and toes.

There are dances for men

POLYNESIAN WAR DANCE. As in many cultures, the warriors of Polynesia—a group of islands in the Pacific—dance in preparation for battle.

and dances for women.

TURKISH GYPSY
FOLK DANCE.
A playful dance that
celebrates women's
strength. The women
tap finger cymbals as
they dance and tease
the audience.

Animals dance.

TIBETAN YAK DANCE.
The noble yak provides
milk, clothing, and
transportation for
Tibetans. Two men
wear a yak costume
and dance to poke fun
at humans.

Puppets dance.

MEXICAN PUPPETS are carried by little boys who dance for the entertainment of children at birthday parties. The puppets are made by the town's piñata maker.

There are country dances

CONTRA DANCING was called country dancing in England. Dancers switch partners as they move up and down the line. Families gather at BARN DANCES to dance the Texas two-step.

and city dances.

BREAK DANCING began on the streets and playgrounds of the inner cities. Young men try to outdo each other with acrobatic movements to hip-hop music.

There are dances that tell stories.

CLASSIC NORTH INDIAN DANCES tell stories. The dancers depict the characters of a story with mime—changes of facial expressions and poses.

One day, the jealous god Indra demanded that the villagers bring him the offerings they were taking to the god Krishna. Old and young, the villagers followed his orders.

Krishna appeared and told the villagers to bring him the gifts as they always did.

When Indra heard of this, he became very angry and shot his arrows into the sky, which caused rain and lightning to appear.

The rains soon flooded the village and the mountain. People tried to swim away from the rising waters.

Krishna appeared. He raised the mountain on his pinkie and saved the people and the village.

Some dances are performed on stage.

THE NUTCRACKER BALLET is a Christmas story about a little girl who gets a magic nutcracker that turns into a prince. He takes her to a magic land of dancers, snowflakes, and sugarplum fairies.

And even if you can't walk, you can still dance.

Most people dance to have fun

and to share happy feelings.